PAGE PUBLISHING Conneaut Lake, PA
First originally published by Page Publishing 2023
ISBN 978-1-6624-8249-6 (pbk) ISBN 978-1-6624-8251-9 (digital)
Printed in the United States of America

IMPRACTICAL JUSTICE

First edition. April 21, 2024.

ISBN: 979-8224540853

Written by Torella Elaine.

This is a book based on the justice system in the State of New Jersey. The wrongful convictions of innocent men who are convicted by the real criminals who practice negligence in criminal proceedings. The conspiracy hidden behind smoke screens that you don't see until it's far too late.

This book brings you up close and personal to real situations that real people go through within the criminal justice system as a result from malpractice. Malpractice that has been transpiring for decades and still exists today.

When you watch the news and see innocent people being released from prison after doing decades of their life behind the wall, it's not a gimmick. The question is, why? Who's responsible? Is it racism? How often do you see any other race outside of Negros who were wrongfully convicted and released after serving majority of their lives in prison?

Take a walk with me as I take you on a journey through the impractical justice of the justice system.

Warning Disclaimer

This book is designed to open the minds of people. Court rules, rules of evidence, criminal practice and procedures, or even the US Constitution are references for you to search on your own. The author is *not* a licensed practitioner of the law. This book is *not* to be taken as legal advice to substitute an attorney. It is more of a guidebook to assist you and open the eyes of those who can't see what's going on right in their face.

The author and publisher specifically disclaims any liability of loss in any form from the use of this book.

This book is dedicated to every man or woman incarcerated in the prison system. I understand your pain and discomfort because I am currently amongst you. I'm in the struggle with you, fighting day in and day out.

It is also dedicated to those of you in society who view law enforcement as innocent and honest people. When the truth is, not every smiling face is friendly, and not every person with a badge means you well. This book is dedicated to unity, equal opportunity, justice, and power to all people!

Just Let Me Vent

Inside the darkest place of the judicial system

is where I currently reside facing life in prison...

mixed emotions and scattered thoughts from an abundance of individuals

control the dynamic of the prison code of ethics that you see in hard criminals...

I often find myself thinking more so for others,

because actions driven from emotions mixed with petty thoughts equals bloodshed amongst brothers...

Brother,

these senseless battles enable trust to win the real war being waged against us,

where state counsels have immunity to wrongfully convict and imprison us...

and judges abuse their discretion with weapons of what you believe is precedent,

but really it's just unpublished court opinions that hold no merit...

unless you challenge the language used in the context,

you're basically giving up on life because you refuse to use your intellect...

Intellect,

we wrongfully use to scheme and cause deceit amongst our own kind,

killing each other physically and morally according to what the masters had in mind...

My mind,

my mind is an intellectual energy not being confined by no binds,

I often think outside of the box because that box too was created by mankind...

My kind,

my kind is not of that kind...

so let's rewind the fact that,

that box is inside of their box which is not of my kind...

so why would I let a boxed thinker dictate and confine the intellectual energy of my mind?

I told you my intellectual energy can't be confined by those binds!

you strive to think outside the box and I strive to think within this galaxy,

because living in this world and not being of it is causing me to be an introvert because you people are

nagging!

They say only God can judge us,

but judges are doing one hell of a job to uphold impractical justice...

and you're an offender of the state who happens to be labeled a defender seeking help from the public?

like those public defenders don't get paid close to nothing to send you up shits creek because they're

impractical about their salary to practice fighting for justice!

you got to be kidding me if you think justice is within this system of impractical convictions to imprison

us,

none of it makes sense,

it's just flat-out ridiculous!

metal walls and concrete floors has become the normality,

so my future seems just as hard and cold as the metal bars that has me kept in captivity...

when I look through these bars I see a mental institution,

mentally unbalanced brothers who were fully prosecuted for being incompetent about their future...

so imagine the level of incompetence in the present,

where previously they gave up on future hopes, so mentally they remain lost in my presence...

My presence,

my presence is often taken for granted...

my presence is often taken for granted by those who left me stranded,

and those who left me stranded often ask for a helping hand when their plans don't go according to

planning...

that's when they suddenly grasp an understanding,

and understand that my presence shouldn't be taken for granted...

I'm an introvert that needed a vent to vent in,

so I chose to vent through the craft of paper meets pen...

I dwell alone in the land where the lost men went,

carrying my own pain and discomfort until my heartbeat ends...

Chapter 1

The Negro Revolution
The revolution starts mentally,
and if you want to become a revolutionary,
you start by overthrowing the self-hate mentality.

Last year in 2020, 1,021 people were shot and killed by police officers. Sworn officers who were placed in our society to protect and serve. When you turn the news on, you see Negros, black people, who are being choked or shot to death.

When was the last time you've seen a man or woman from the Caucasian race on the news because he or she was accidentally choked to death by law enforcement? Brutally assaulted by law enforcement? Or shot to death by law enforcement, who happens to be a Negro officer?

Could you imagine the backlash that officer and many other Negros would receive? Could you imagine the extent they (White America) would go to prosecute the Negro officer? Do you really think a resolution could have been found without an act of revolution if 1,021 Caucasians were murdered by Negro officers?

A knee was placed on a brother's neck named George Floyd by an officer in Minnesota, who kept his knee there for a handful of minutes after he stopped breathing. The brother was handcuffed, lying on his stomach, and kept repeating the words "I can't breathe" until he actually stopped breathing. Is that justice practical or impractical? If you believe that was practical justice, then you are a racist!

The time is now. Because it has been the time for some time that a revolution is needed! The mess has to get cleaned up. Order needs to be installed, and visions need to change. The Negro revolution is needed so the corruption, death, and mass incarceration of Negros can be impeded.

What Is a Revolution?

According to Merriam Webster's Collegiate Dictionary, Eleventh Edition,

> 2 a: a sudden, radical, or complete change b: a fundamental change in political organization; esp: the overthrow or renunciation of one government or ruler and the substitution of another by the governed c: activity or movement designed to effect fundamental changes in the socioeconomic situation d: a fundamental change in the way of thinking about or visualizing something.

What Is a Revolutionary?

> 1 a of, or relating to, or constituting a revolution <war> b: tending to or promoting revolution c: constituting or bringing about a major or fundamental change.

Brothers and sisters, we need change, and we need people to unite to make that change, but that change has to start with *us* first! We have to clean up our own backyards and do some spring cleaning of the heart, mind, body, and soul before we can make a change in this land.

In this land, the word *revolution* is frowned upon. Being a revolutionary makes you a terrorist of some sort. What about white supremacy? Are they labeled as a terrorist group? Do you hear of the FBI infiltrating their organization and doing to them what happened to Fred Hampton and many others? The answer is no.

I'll say again that, the word *revolution* is frowned upon, and being a revolutionary makes you a terrorist of some sort. Ironically, there are a great number of Christians in this world who will read this book and have a bad taste in their mouth about my personal views on social engineering. Those same Christians read a book called The Bible (Basic

Instructions Before Leaving Earth). In that Bible is a man named Jesus. Jesus was in fact a revolutionary, and Jesus believed in revolution.

Jesus preached and personally spoke to the people, giving them the Word of God. When Jesus spoke, it was to make "a sudden, radical, or complete change b: a fundamental change in political organization; esp: the overthrow or renunciation of one government or ruler and the substitution of another by the governed c: activity or movement designed to effect fundamental changes in the socioeconomic situation d: a fundamental change in the way of thinking about or visualizing something."

Now because this man Jesus believed in revolution, his actions were the actions of a revolutionary, which makes him a revolutionary himself! Why? Because his everyday movement was dedicated to "tending to or promoting revolution c: constituting or bringing about a major or fundamental change."

According to the Bible, guess who else believed in revolution and was also an extreme revolutionary? God! Why do you think Noah built the ark? God felt as though a sudden, radical, or complete change was needed on planet Earth. So God sent a flood and killed everything that wasn't on Noah's ark. Which makes God himself a revolutionary. Why? Because God was "tending to or promoting revolution c: constituting or bringing about a major or fundamental change."

Isn't it safe to say that all prophets believe in revolution and are considered revolutionaries to some extent? Go against the Islamic community and see if they believe in revolution. Try the Catholics, Christians, Jehovah Witnesses, etc. and see if you find revolutionaries.

It is only frowned upon when a Negro man or woman says they're a revolutionary, and it's time for a revolution! Too many Negros in one setting, and all on the same page "is always considered a threat, especially if those Negros are not kept on a leash!"

*****

Recently I've watched one of the many news channels who've aired the Capitol being under attack. Those were mostly people of the Caucasian race who believed they were actually doing what a former president of this country wanted them to do. Mostly people of the Caucasian race and a sprinkle of house Negros here and there.

The police didn't kill not one of them. They didn't beat the hell out of not one. What puzzled me the most was the brother. There was a Negro officer whom I assumed worked in the Capitol. He had a nightstick, I believe, and maybe a department-issued weapon. I'm not sure. I also don't see why he wouldn't have one working in that field.

In any event, he was being chased up the stairs and through the hallways after repeatedly giving direct orders to these Caucasian people to "stop." They ignored all his commands and continued to pursue him as if almost to dare him to do something other than to run away. I couldn't believe my eyes! I was looking at the television almost anticipating to see gunfire or to hear about the death of terrorists at the Capitol.

You know what, I did, and they were all innocent people who were under attack. Not one of them were intruders. I saw pictures on the news of people all through the Capitol. Tearing that place up! Some carried flags, some had weapons, and one of the gentlemen had the audacity to have his feet on someone's desk. The people who were apprehended, when asked, said they did what they thought the president of the United States at that time wanted them to do.

Imagine if a bunch of Negros (whether field or house) would have gathered together and ambushed the Capitol, killing four to five innocent people, taking selfies (pictures), and saying we were doing what we thought Barack Obama wanted us to do? Opposed to the four or five innocent lives that were lost, there would have been Negros dying by the dozens. Magazines from assault rifles emptied, reloaded, and emptied again into the crowds of Negros.

The police would have taken more Negro lives in that one day than COVID-19 took in a week, and COVID is a bad muthafucka! When

I saw this event, I thought to myself, *There is no privilege, like a white privilege, 'cause a white privilege is supreme.* No wonder them people believe in white supremacy.

The situation at hand is, we are *not* equal. We were brought to this land to be enslaved, and not much has changed. The struggle has just been modernized. Those seeds of segregation that were planted in our minds many decades ago was a mental warfare being waged against *us.*

Instead of plantations, you now have prisons. Prisons that pay prisoners close to nothing. I'm myself a head cook at Trenton State Prison. I cook for about 1,300 prisoners a day, seven days a week, on an eight-hour shift. There are no days off. You're only entitled to one day off a year, and that's on your birthday.

I get paid $3.20 a day—$3.20 a day multiplied by thirty days a month is $96.00 a month. After the fines I pay from court fees, I'll receive $60.00 a month, and $60.00 a month times twelve months is $720.00 a year. Everything we buy off commissary has a 10 percent tax rate. Sneakers, boxers, socks, food, batteries, radio, etc. What cook do you know in society that works part-time, at any diner or fast-food spot that makes $720.00 a year? Nobody out there works overtime without being paid for it. You know why? Because it's illegal. In prison, it's not illegal because nobody cares about us, and it's a plantation. It's considered a punishment and a form of us paying our debt to society. It's slavery, and slavery is permitted when you're in prison. Where's the fundamental fairness in that?

Amendment XIII 1865

Section 1

Neither slavery nor involuntary servitude, except as a punishment for crime whereof the party shall have been duly convicted, shall exist within the United States, or any place subject to their jurisdiction.

*****

You've just read the Thirteenth Amendment of the United States Constitution. You can see it, as clear as day, that when you get convicted of a crime, slavery or involuntary servitude is permitted. So again I'll say, plantations were replaced with prisons.

The structure has changed physically

to be modernized with the times, however,

the infrastructure mentally has not changed at all.

Another seed of segregation that was placed in our minds is self-hate. We have to stop practicing self-hate and hate for one another for *us* to unite and love each other. We are the only race of people who actually embrace the derogatory name that was given to *us* by our oppressors. Nigger! That's my nigga. Yo nigga! Fuck that nigga! Me and my niggas!

Have you ever heard a Mexican do that? Wet back! That's my wet back! Yo wet back! Me and my wet backs! What about Puerto Ricans, Caucasians, etc. None of these people embrace the names cracker, honkey, or spic. Just as well as the police don't embrace the name pig. So why do we?

This mindset is ignorant! There is nothing prideful about referring to another brother or ourselves with this form of hate, whether it be a conscious statement or not. Many of you will say to yourselves, "I'm not a hater!" Well, when *our* oppressors were raping *our* women, beating *our* ancestors half to death with whips, lynching *our* black men, selling *our* children, working *us* in the cotton fields on the plantation, and feeding *us* scraps that today you wouldn't even feed your dog, they called *us* what? Nigger! Dirty nigger! Black and ugly nigger! Do you think when they used that word, it came from a place of love or hate?

Just a few moments ago, literally, I stopped writing this for a short break. I ran this idea past an associate of mine who happened to stop at my cell this morning. His input on the matter was, "Yes we were given a derogatory name that our oppressors used to degrade *us*, and yes it came from a place of hate, but we didn't let that word hold *us* down. We adopted that word and now wear it as a badge of honor."

My response was, I disagree. I disagree because it is not a badge of honor. It is a negative seed that was planted into *our* minds to manipulate *our* people. There are a great number of brothers and sisters who believe that black is ugly. I don't want that black ass nigga. What I'm a do with that black ass bitch? No, no, he/she is too dark for me. I can't be seen with him/her.

We were taught to hate *our* people and *ourselves*. We hate what we are and where we come from! Our people frown upon the brothers and sisters who are in Africa or who come to America from Africa. We have become so Americanized that *we* feel as though *we* are better than what *we* originate from. We hate *our* identity! We hate *our* history! We look down on the people who come from the land that birthed *our* ancestors! That is self-hate! We have been manipulated, whether you want to accept the truth or not. This is what it is. Our people are brainwashed!

More often than not, our people make music pertaining to us selling drugs to our people. Using guns with extended magazines to kill our own people. We make music degrading our beautiful black women. This has to stop! We need to respect our women and let our women know that they have great value and that is why they are valued.

Listen, when we go to jail, we can't depend on brothers from our so-called block, that we don't own. That black woman is by your side though. Answering your collect calls, coming to visits, sending you money for commissary, and making court appearances. That's who has your back! A black woman! Who changed your diapers? Who fed you? Who bathed you? Who put clothes on your back? Who wiped your little sorry tears and told you, "Baby, it'll be okay"? When you can't man up, take care of your child, or you happen to go to prison, who takes on that responsibility by themselves? A woman! That's who.

So how dare you mimic a damn fool who has no respect for what you need at your lowest point? That is not an idol, and that person is nothing to idolize. That person is brainwashed, prideful, lost, ignorant, and doing exactly what the puppet masters want him to do. Create music to degrade black people. They'll all dance to it, mimic it, and you'll mentally give birth to another inspiring asshole filled with ignorance to follow suit. You are a *house Negro*!

Our people make music talking about killing one another. The kids at home listen to this self-hate music, and they pick up guns. When they pick up guns, guess who they shoot? Exactly who America wants you to shoot—each other. Yes, you too are house Negros!

You're doing exactly what Master wants you to do. Field Negros didn't do that. If you say you're not a *house Negro*, then do what Master doesn't want you to do.

I challenge you to

1. educate yourselves,
2. educate each other,
3. love yourself,
4. love one another,
5. help one another,
6. call someone you have problems with and forgive them,
7. unite with your people and stop the senseless segregation,
8. listen and respect the wisdom of your elders,
9. learn the laws of this land,
10. teach these laws to one another,
11. support black-owned businesses,
12. stop practicing self-hate, and

13. use your voice for something positive.

*****

The Negro revolution starts in our mind! Information was kept from us in books. They didn't want us to learn to read. They wanted us to be illiterate. Knowledge is power! Obtain that power by obtaining knowledge.

We as people need a fundamental change in the way we think about ourselves, others, and life. Then we need to act on those fundamental changes of the mind to better ourselves as men and women. We need to teach the revolution to our children as well. I'm talking to all ethnic backgrounds at this point. We all need to unite for equal opportunity, justice, and power to all people!

Chapter 2

Learning Your Rights
If you learn your rights,
then you know what you're fighting for
and why you're fighting for it.

Learning your rights can be a very complex or simplistic thing. It all depends on the individual. How bad you want to learn it and how profound you want your knowledge to be in this field. Being that your rights is such a broad topic, we'll keep it simple because all the information on your rights cannot fit in this book.

History is very important. Many of us as people do not know the history behind the law, the Constitution, or any amendments within the Constitution. This lack of knowledge is what makes us detrimental to ourselves. We hold ourselves back by not obtaining this fruitful information to assist us in moving forward when the powers that be hold *us* back.

The law is a body of rules established to control the conduct of people in society.

The rule of law is that nobody is above the law.

As simplistic as this sounds, it is very important. One of the reasons is the police enforce a body of rules which make up the law. They enforce *the law* but, *the rule of law* is that nobody is above *the law*.

Let's discuss the police in our communities. First, I want to start off by saying, not all cops are bad cops. The problem is, 90 percent, if not more, will cover up injustice they witness other cops do to people in society. So I pose the question of, do police protect and serve, or do they protect each other as they serve injustice in our communities?

More often than not, *our* people do not know their constitutional rights. They also are unaware of civil suits they can file against the police for harassment, violation of due process, illegal search and seizure, etc. This is why learning the law of the land is very vital.

In my opinion, technology was a blessing! Nobody believed us when we cried out for years that the police were corrupt! They were the criminals! They framed people! They would beat the black off you! They would kill you! Nobody believed us!

Now we have cell phones with cameras. We have police wearing body cameras, and everybody is recording these tragic events. It's all over the news and social media. America has just begun to believe that racism actually still exists! There are many innocent Caucasians who are naive to this fact. They simply did not know. Not anymore though. It has now become public.

You now see Caucasians marching with us in the middle of the pandemic. You see them protesting, getting pepper sprayed, screaming "Black lives matter!" at the top of their lungs, going face to face with the police in the middle of the streets right along with us!

They can't believe what's going on. They never thought this type of stuff is in existence. They do now though, and now that they have knowledge of this, do you know what they believe in? *Revolution!* Not just any revolution but *the Negro revolution*! They believe in equal opportunity, justice, and power to all people!

They believe in these things because they now see that police are not who and what they believed them to be. They now see that police are murdering people, in cold blood, for no reason at all, and getting away with it time and time again. These relentless actions they partake in are demonic, uncivilized, and cruel.

Think about this, body cameras have exposed police brutality. These police are wearing body cameras, so you know they're putting some shade on their actions compared to prior incidents. Now, if they're putting shade on their actions and their body cameras show them shooting unarmed people, imagine what they were doing to us before body cameras came into existence. Some of the things they did to our people is a lot worse than dying. In other words, some people would rather die than to relive those experiences again.

I suggest everyone who reads this book learns the state and United States Constitution. If you are incarcerated, the facility you are housed at has a law library. Use it! If you can afford a *Black's Law Dictionary*, purchase one. If you are in society, then I recommend you use Google or simply go to the public library and learn as much as you can.

Don't be selfish with this information. Share it with people. Share it with your children, siblings, parents, friends, and anyone else who will listen. Knowledge is power!

Again, your rights is a very broad topic to discuss. You have the following:

Bill of Rights	Patent rights	Vested rights
Common rights	Petition of rights	
Declaration of rights	Private rights	Natural rights
Exclusive rights	Right heir	Civil rights
Marital rights	Riparian rights	Constitutional rights
Mere rights	Stock rights	

Right. As a noun, and taken in an abstract sense, means justice, ethical correctness, or consonance with the rules of law or the principles of morals. Rights are defined as "powers of free action."

Constitutional right. A right guaranteed to the citizens by the United States Constitution and state constitutions and so guaranteed as to prevent legislative interference therewith.

Constitutional freedom. Generic term to describe the basic freedoms guaranteed by the Constitution such as the First Amendment freedoms of religion, speech, press, and assembly together with protection under due process clause of the Fourteenth Amendment.

Bill of Rights. First ten Amendments to US Constitution providing for individual rights, freedoms, and protections.

Black's Law Dictionary Sixth Edition

First Ten Amendments

First Amendment. Amendment to US Constitution guaranteeing basic freedoms of speech, religion, press, and assembly and the right to petition the government for redress of grievances.

Second Amendment. The Second Amendment to the US Constitution provides that a well-regulated militia, being necessary to the security of a free state, the right of the people to keep and bear arms shall not be infringed. State and federal laws however regulate the sale, transportation, and possession of firearms.

Third Amendment. No soldier shall, in time of peace, be quartered in any house, without the consent of the owner, nor in time of war, but in a manner to be prescribed by law.

Fourth Amendment. Guaranteeing people the right to be secure in their homes and property against unreasonable searches and seizures and providing that no warrants shall issue except upon probable cause and then only as to specific places to be searched and persons and things to be seized.

Fifth Amendment. Providing that no person shall be required to answer for a capital or otherwise infamous offense unless on indictment or presentment of a grand jury except in military cases; that no person will suffer double jeopardy; that no person will be compelled to be a witness against himself; that no person shall be deprived of life, liberty, or property without due process of law; and that private property will not be taken for public use without just compensation.

Sixth Amendment. Includes such rights as the right to speedy and public trial by an impartial jury, right to be informed of the nature of the accusation, the right to confront witnesses, the right to assistance of counsel and compulsory process.

Seventh Amendment. In suit at common law, where the value in controversy shall exceed twenty dollars, the right of trial by jury shall be preserved, and no fact tried by a jury shall be otherwise reexamined in any court of the United States, than according to the rules of the common law.

Eighth Amendment. Prohibits excessive bail, excessive fines, and cruel and unusual punishment.

Ninth Amendment. The enumeration in the Constitution, of certain rights, shall not be construed to deny or disparage others retained by the people.

Tenth Amendment. The powers not delegated to the United States by the Constitution, nor prohibited by it to the States, are reserved to the States respectively or to the people.

These are the first ten amendments to your constitutional rights. There are others within the United States Constitution, but in this book, we'll only address these ten.

Example

Let's say, for example, you or someone you live with has a warrant out for their arrest, for child support, robbery, theft, whatever. When the police come to your home, they must have a warrant. That warrant must be signed by a judge, and it also must determine what the police are allowed to search.

If the police have a body warrant for whomever, there is no need to open dresser drawers, the refrigerator, remove cushions from couches, open cabinets, etc. A human being can't fit in any of those places.

So if the police come to your home with a body warrant, and they find a weapon, drugs, or anything in your cabinet, they have violated the Fourth Amendment of your constitutional rights. Why? Because it was an illegal search and seizure.

Also the violation of the due process clause, procedural, in which a person is guaranteed fair procedures and substantive which protects a person's property from unfair governmental interference.

The Fifth Amendment of your constitutional rights protects you from this as well. The reason why is the police would have violated the fair procedure of how the warrant was supposed to be carried out.

The body warrant did not warrant them to open your cabinet. Whatever they find in your home, you cannot be charged with because they have violated the rights you are protected by.

Ironically, the police are crafty. Some of them will conduct the illegal search, and once they find something, then they'll request a warrant to further search the premises. That way they'll further tie you into an indictment. Some will even plant something in your home and say it was yours. It's your word against law enforcement. Who do you think the jury will believe if you go to trial?

This is just one minor impractical justice that goes on in urban communities or Negro homes in America. The good thing is, technology. The cameras on cell phones can be used to obtain evidence that can support your claim made against the police.

If you know your rights, then you know what you're fighting for and why you're fighting for it. Many of us hire private attorneys or obtain counsel from the Public Defender's Office. Once we receive either, more often than not, we tend to ease up and let the attorney do their job.

In my opinion, that is the most selfless decision for anyone facing criminal charges to make. It is your life. It is your freedom. Why wouldn't you learn the rules to the game? You should want to fight tooth and nail with your attorney to get the outcome you desire. If not, then you should get comfortable. Because your freedom isn't of any value to you, and you're only contributing to the cause of the oppressors.

You are not a fighter. You are not for the *revolution*. You are and, with the same mentality, always will be a *house Negro*!

Chapter 3

Grand Jury: Bias or Not

The criminal justice system is a systematic structure
set in place to maintain the infrastructure of slavery.

When you are arrested for a claim made against you, before you can be charged, the matter must be brought in front of a grand jury to determine if you'll actually be indicted. Before you get indicted, legally you are not charged with anything.

Now when the claims made against you go in front of a grand jury to determine if you'll actually be charged, you are not allowed to be present. (At least in the State of New Jersey.) The prosecution presents their side of the story. Whatever they say to the grand jury is going unchallenged because you're not permitted to be present. Your attorney can be present, but "he/she is not permitted to intervene."

You cannot be present at the grand jury proceedings to testify on your own behalf unless the prosecutor gives you consent. The very person who is trying to bury you in prison has the power to determine if they want you to testify on your own behalf in front of the grand jury. That's insane.

How is this procedure fundamentally fair in any event? Everyone gets indicted because the suspect/defendant doesn't get a chance to combat the allegations made against him/her. It is a totally biased proceeding that guarantees everyone to get indicted.

In other words, it's a systematic structure set in place to maintain the infrastructure of slavery. Plantations have been transformed into prisons. Slaves in prison generate more revenue than slaves on a plantation. Especially with the jobs inside of prison that manufacture things for society and the taxes we pay on everything we need to survive.

Plus it's legal in every state of the United States of America. If we didn't do any jobs within the prison, an outside source would have to be hired by the state to come in and work for a decent salary or hourly rate. It's cheaper to enslave prisoners and pay them $60 a month as opposed to a salary of $60,000 a year.

Also in this proceeding, who can you trust to properly screen the jury? You think the judge or prosecutor has your best interest at heart? What if one of the jury members is an ex-boyfriend or girlfriend? What if two of the jury members are best friends or family members to two of your ex-boyfriends or girlfriends? The prosecutor will not know! The judge won't either! It's biased, and the odds are stacked against you.

Someone made a claim against you, you get arrested, you can't defend yourself against being indicted unless your opposition allows it, publicly your character is assassinated in all local newspapers, and your sitting in the county jail oblivious to the fact that you've already been thrown into the systematic structure to maintain the infrastructure of slave trading.

I personally have never seen my grand jury transcripts for any indicted offenses I've had. Every time I've asked an attorney, they'll ask me, "Why?" I'll give them an answer, and they'll never get around to it. The problem is, it's too much work for them, and attorneys believe in working smarter, not harder.

Many are overwhelmed with caseloads or simply don't care to accommodate your concerns. In their minds, you're incompetent. You don't know the law. That's why you hired them. Shut up and let them do their job. Absolutely not! You're entitled to grand jury transcripts. Your attorney has a copy on disk.

Why grand jury transcripts are essential

The grand jury transcripts are very important. The jurors' names are present in these transcripts. You'll have a chance to comb through these transcripts to see if you know the jurors. (Remember, they could be enemies of yours.) See if any biased things stand out to you. Did the prosecutor lie and present false accusations to get you indicted? Did the judge overlook vital information that, if corrected, would have prevented you from getting indicted?

You won't know until you get the grand jury transcripts and read them. Once you read them, you'll still need to read the rules governing the courts to get an idea of the procedure, who may be present, the defendant's rights, interpreter's presence, rights of private citizens, secrecy of proceedings, objections to grand jury and grand jurors, objects to the array, among many other things.

If you don't read, you'll never know.

If you never know, you'll never fight.

If you do fight, it'll be for all the wrong reasons,

and the ends won't justify the means.

You are a paycheck, not a close friend or family member to your attorney. Speak up, learn your rights, read the rules governing the courts, criminal practice and procedure, rules of evidence. Learn cases similar to yours, read the United States Constitution and the state constitution, and when you're in court, speak up to put things on the record. Do not bite your tongue! It is your life! Not your attorney's!

Many attorneys will disregard what you have to say. They don't have time, and they were not hired to be legal teachers to people with a desire to be students of the law. They were hired to get you out of a jam. Try not to waste their time with fruitless information and questions. They don't have the time!

Chapter 4

The Smoke Screen Conspiracies

It's your responsibility to learn the law. The judge doesn't care if you're ignorant to the depths of the procedure. The law is public information. It is not anyone's fault but your own if you don't understand the law, the procedures, the rules, and your rights.

If you can't afford a private attorney, then you'll be appointed counsel from the Public Defender's Office or a pool attorney. I want to assist you in a more profound way of viewing public defenders. They are humans! Not superheroes!

It's 365 days in a year. That's 52 weeks. Christmas, New Year's, Thanksgiving, weekends, etc. Let's take 7 weeks off for holidays. (That's a very generous number!) So 52 weeks - 7 weeks is 45 weeks. Courts are closed on the weekends. Friday and Saturday is 2 days a week times 52 weeks = 104 days. That's about 3 1/2 months which = 14 weeks. We have 45 weeks - 14 weeks = 32 weeks. Then 32 weeks = about 8 months. This number doesn't include sick days or vacation time.

You are only one client. There is an abundance of you who are indigent and need public assistance. Some are petty crimes and others, felonies. Some take plea offers, and others go to trial. Their clients are constantly rotating, and you're just another face with the same story as everyone else. "I'm not guilty," and then you plead guilty when an offer is presented.

Do you really think they have the time to dedicate all their energy into one client? Absolutely not! These people are not robots. They actually have a life outside of the courtroom. Their children and/or parents get sick and catch common colds right along with them. They deal with stress, anxiety, depression, distraught, and anger, just like other humans do. They are not the magicians or robots you want them to be.

The public defenders get paid on a salary. Some care very deeply about their clients because they care deeply about their own personal career. These are the ones who want to open their own law firm.

Some great public defenders do exist. They are just a rare breed. Those are the ones who stay at the Public Defender's Office because they know, without their assistance, many people who are indigent will be in a bad place.

Your Attorney

Your attorney in criminal matters is supposed to protect you from claims made against you. They place the duty on the state (prosecution) to prove that you are guilty of whatever claim made against you. If your indictment is taking too long, your attorney can file a motion to dismiss for failure to indict.

Once you are indicted and receive discoveries, you will then know the evidence the state has against you. Your attorney will read these discoveries and begin to dissect the evidence, the procedures followed to obtain the evidence, the witnesses, the inconsistent statements, the identification, the procedure followed to obtain an identification among many other things. It all depends on your situation.

After these things are accomplished, your attorney can or will put in motions to challenge the evidence. If the motions are granted by the court, you'll have a hearing. At that hearing, your attorney will have the privilege of questioning the witnesses in court to establish a record, learn more about the case, the witnesses, and possibly weaken the claim made against you.

The Prosecutor

The prosecutor has a duty to seek justice and not to merely convict. Unfortunately, that is not the case, in my opinion.

The prosecutors work with detectives every day. These same detectives are the ones who investigate the claim made against you. They do the identification procedure. They interview all the witnesses. They type the probable cause for your arrest, and the judge signs off on it. Until or if you even go to trial, they feel as though their job is complete.

Most of us don't know the law. We don't know procedures, what we're entitled to, or what isn't supposed to happen. Detectives know this. They also know that majority of us who get arrested can't afford private counsel, we won't learn the law, and we'll nine times out of ten take a deal the state offers.

So they aren't concerned about coming to court anytime soon for a pretrial proceeding. Which gives the detectives, sergeants, and police a nice blind spot to do a bunch of things that go against the Fifth and Fourteenth Amendments of the US Constitution.

Now when they do have to come to court, guess who covers up all the dirty tricks? The prosecutors! They are aware of all the dirty tricks that transpired leading to your arrest. They are aware of the suggestiveness, leading questions, mandated attorney general guidelines that weren't followed, etc. So what do they do? The opposite of seeking justice and not merely to obtain convictions. They seek conviction, because conviction is their justice.

How often do you hear a state's attorney say, "I don't want to prosecute the defendant because my understanding of the police department and the detectives in this matter is that they're all corrupted." I've never seen it! The only time something close to this transpires is when the state's attorney tries everything in their power to tap dance around the misconduct.

Once the pretrial motions transpire and the prosecutor can see their witnesses are not solid enough mentally to take the stand, they will then still try to obtain a conviction by getting you to accept a deal that you can't refuse.

That is not justice. That is not the duty of the state's attorney, but that is exactly what transpires in the United States of America.

The Judge

They are the referee of the legal fight between the accused and the accuser. They're supposed to work with proper dignity and fairness. Protect the defendant's rights and preserving the public interest at the same time. What a position to uphold.

The judge will be fully aware that something isn't right but will do nothing about it. I've witnessed judges tell the prosecutor, "It's your case, try it as you may."

There was a prior case I had, and the defense attorney and myself were at a 404 (b) hearing / in limine motion. The state wanted to bring in other crime evidence of other bad acts. The state's witnesses were horrible, and their stories didn't provide clear and convincing evidence.

They admitted they didn't know me. They admitted other people gave them a description of me. They further admitted we'd never had a conversation, they'd never seen a picture of me, and we had never been in the same room before.

Needless to say, we (the defense) actually won that in limine motion. The problem was the ruling of the court. The court ruled that, although the defense won the motion, we could not use the witnesses' statements against them at trial. That would be considered opening the door to other crime evidence.

The court also gave strict instructions to the state's counsel not to bring any of this into trial because "the state's motion to admit evidence on 404 (b) is denied in its entirety."

So here I am at trial months later unable to defend myself because the court made a ruling stripping me of a fundamentally fair trial. My attorney at the time said we had to walk a tightrope because of the ruling. I couldn't use their lies against them to show the jury these people were compulsive liars. The prosecutor didn't walk a tightrope at all. Every underhanded trick he could pull was pulled.

Even when objections were made by the defense and the court sustained the objections. The real problem was, the jury already heard the damaging information. Once they heard it, it was locked in their minds. It was not going anywhere!

Does that sound like the prosecutor was seeking justice, or does it sound like the prosecutor wanted to merely convict? Does that sound like the judge wanted to protect the defendant's rights or preserve the interest of the state?

Let's be clear. The public doesn't know the law. The public only knows that a terrible event transpired and someone is in custody for it. If the police and prosecutors went through the trouble of bringing you into court, selecting a jury, calling in witnesses, and making the jury deliberate on the matter, you must be guilty!

That is how a large percentage of them think. Some will admit it, and others won't. During jury selection, many of them will admit it, and the judge will excuse them with cause. It's the ones who think like this and won't say anything that'll bury you in prison.

These are the things people don't address and society doesn't hear about. Since society is unaware of it, it simply doesn't exist to them. If it doesn't exist to the masses, who will or could be a voice on the outside to advocate for people behind the wall? That has to change!

*****

So your attorney is defending you.

The question is, what standard are they being held to?

The ABA (American Bar Association) is defined in the *Black's Law Dictionary* as a national association of lawyers; a primary purpose of which is the improvement of lawyers' services and the administration of justice. Membership in the ABA is open to any lawyer who is in good standing in his or her state.

Basically people who work together or who have known each other for decades. They are not throwing each other under the bus when they witness or hear about a misconduct. These are judges, lawyers, and prosecutors. You have to do some really outrageous, selfish, bona fide stupid action that sheds light on everyone who plays in the dark for them to expose you. How often do you think that happens?

Breaking News

Today, which is April 20, 2021, officer Derek Chauvin was found guilty of all charges in the death of George Perry Floyd Jr.—second-degree unintentional murder, third-degree murder, and second-degree manslaughter. Today is more than just a National Smoke Day. Today the blue silence of police officers has been broken. A Caucasian officer was found guilty on all charges for murdering a Negro! That is justice! And this is the beginning!

*****

RPC is known as Rules of Professional Conduct. They govern attorneys just as well as the Ethics Committee. The problem is, if you don't learn the rules to the game, how can you play it? You have to know the rules to know what standard to hold your lawyer to. If you don't know what they're supposed to do and what they're not supposed to do, then you don't know anything. If you don't know anything, you're subject to anything, and that is a terrible thing.

So the prosecutors interview witnesses. They prep witnesses for motions. They ask the witnesses questions and tell them what to say. They inform them of what the defense attorney will ask. They also inform them on how to get out of those questions. Their infamous line, "I don't recall," is always used when your attorney asks a question the state's witness doesn't want to answer.

Let us dissect this scenario for a second. You have a prosecutor who merely wants to convict. They work hand in hand with detectives to merely convict. Detectives and prosecutors use leading questions to lead the witness in directions they want them to travel.

Your attorney attacks the witnesses on cross-examination. He/she attacks the credibility of detectives and experts who testify.

The prosecutors use case law and the rules of evidence to navigate their arguments, for example, to the exception to hearsay. If you or your attorney don't know these rules, how to persuade the judge to see your vision of this rule, how to counter these rules with other case laws or some other updated rule of evidence, then you are in bad shape.

The smoke screen conspiracy is, you really think that when you go to court, the judge, prosecutor, and lawyer you've obtained are going to play by the rules and make sure justice is served.

No! They'll play by rules that you don't know. They'll use legal terms that you don't understand. The judge will make a ruling that will be dead wrong, and it will affect the entire outcome of your case, but you'll go to trial, lose, and then wait three or four years to get your appeal answered by the appellate division.

You'll be traded like chattel, while others in position get a paycheck. Then you'll be placed on a plantation (prison). There, you will be treated like a slave and fed like an animal. Because in the beginning, you couldn't see through the smoke screen to know that you were victimized by a conspiracy. A systematic procedure to enslave others and make a fortune.

Chapter 5

Smoke Screen Conspiracies II

We're not even officially charged with a crime until we're indicted. Prior to that, we're just being accused. So how is it that our life, liberty, and property are being infringed upon without due process of law being essential? How can the state infringe upon your constitutional right that was given to you after the Civil War, to protect us as "black people" who are liberated from slavery, to embrace citizenship? How are we liberated to embrace citizenship if an accusation without an indictment can result in our life, liberty, and property being infringed upon?

Recently I asked someone who is confined amongst me these same questions. The response he gave me I found out was a very common thought pattern that most people possess. His response was, "We are given due process of law in pretrial proceedings. That's why we have court rules and rules of evidence that we and/or our attorneys are supposed to read and understand to make sure those rules are being held in court."

In my opinion, that is a very shallow and premature thought. My reason for thinking this is Section 1 of the Fourteenth Amendment in the US Constitution states as follows:

> No State shall make or enforce any law which shall abridge the privileges or immunities of citizens of the United States; nor shall any State deprive any person of life, liberty, or property, without due process of law; nor deny to any person within its jurisdiction the equal protection of the laws.

So the problem I'm having with this thought pattern is, a person has already been arrested. At that moment, a person is deprived of his/her liberty. You are no longer free to come and go as you please. Your (property) cell phone, clothes, car keys, etc. is apprehended from you.

You are held until your innocence is proven beyond a reasonable doubt. Unless you choose to plead guilty and accept an offer from the state.

This is a normal procedure that transpires in New Jersey, yet it's contrary to what the US Constitution says we "the citizens" are entitled to.

The key word in the text is *shall*. This is a commanding word. When the Supreme Court uses words like *shall* or *must*, that means it's not up for discussion. This is what is *going* to happen. So when this same language is used in the US Constitution, why isn't it respected?

A response to my thought pattern from the man was, "We are given due process when the detectives obtain probable cause to make the arrest. If you believe the probable cause for your arrest is flawed and you can prove it, then you attack the merit of the probable cause through pretrial motions."

This sounds great on one end, but on the other end, it sounds like you're already caught up in a systematic maze of destruction trying to find your way out with the odds stacked against you. You're already captured by the powers that be. Liberation is now an issue for you.

Think about it

They'll arrest a man/woman from a low-income housing complex and send him/her to the county jail with no bail. It may take a year before an indictment is obtained. Even the grand jury process is biased. Because the accused is no longer liberated to enjoy his/her life and property and cannot be present to defend themselves to obtain rights that never should have been infringed upon in the first place!

How, or better yet why, aren't we protected by the US Constitution in the matter of accusations? If we're not officially charged, we shouldn't be deprived of life, liberty, and property. Why should we be forced to place burdens on our loved ones to accept collect calls, buy commissary, pay lawyer fees, burn gas driving back and forth to visits, and taking off from work just because we were accused of something? Especially when the Fourteenth Amendment prohibits the state from depriving any person of life, liberty, or property without due process of law.

They deprive us then say they'll follow the due process of law to hopefully obtain a conviction. That is not the promise American citizens were guaranteed in the language of the US Constitution.

The Supreme Court needs to interpret this to clarify its official meaning. The legislature needs to create a law to abolish such unconstitutional provisions from transpiring. Especially since it's contrary to what the Constitution promises the citizens of this country.

Another way to view this in my opinion is, the procedural law is shallow. After the Civil War, there were three amendments added to the US Constitution, the thirteenth, fourteenth, and fifteenth. These amendments were added to restrict the powers of state governments and to protect black people, to enjoy the privileges of American citizenship. The Thirteenth Amendment abolishes slavery *unless you are convicted of a crime and sent to prison.*

Thomas Jefferson was the author of the Declaration of Independence and also a Founding Father of the US Constitution. He along with many other Founding Fathers were all slave owners.

So when you look at the Thirteenth Amendment that was added to the US Constitution after the Civil War, are you surprised? I'm not. The Founding Fathers of the US Constitution believed black people were meant to be slaves and white people were meant to reign supreme. These Founding Fathers of the US Constitution were slave masters. They were supreme to their black slaves. I am not surprised that the US Constitution is the supreme law of the land, especially when I take into account who drafted the whole thing.

They did exactly what they believed in, and if you had the power to do so, then you would have done what you believed in. It's nothing more than a loophole that keeps black people in slavery. A devil in a red dress.

It's a secret society that hid right in our face. The Framers and Founders of the US Constitution birthed an elite group (secret society) to run America with an iron fist. These were slave owners! They still possess these elite groups today in 2021, where Supreme Court justices and lawyers treat the law like clay. They formulate what they please out of it with an interpretation that best fits their argument. Their arguments keep minorities held to fill up plantations we now call prisons. *Crafty!*

Before your mind begins to race toward the shallow thoughts of "Black people are not the only ones in prison." I'll further say that common sense should lead one to think the elite group knows there will be casualties. Like a casino, they lose a few and gain a thousand times more. At the end of the day, who reigns supreme?

So back to my point about this shallow rule on due process that is given to us in the Fourteenth Amendment. Judges more often than not sign any warrant that comes in front of them.

Their mentality is, if he/she is innocent, they'll have to prove it in court. After the defendant is apprehended, he/she then awaits for the indictment to be returned. I cannot speak for other states from a standpoint of experience, but in the state of New Jersey, a gallon of milk will get indicted in the drop of a dime (figuratively speaking).

Slavery is one step away from your front door. Just as well as death awaits you at a traffic stop or a local convenience store when you're trying to buy a pack of skittles. What's the difference between a black man being accused and lynched by racist oppressors and a black man being accused and lost in the system for life by racist oppressors? Nothing, except one brings you to an early death, and the latter tortures you mentally and emotionally until the day of your death. Not much has changed.

(This is why I disagree with the shallow mindset of the individual I questioned on the subject matter.)

The US Constitution, as you can see, was established to keep the state in line from oppressing the people. So when you go to court, *State v. Whoever You Are*, keep in mind that the state has a history of infringing upon the rights of people. That's why the federal government has to oversee what they do. If the state was innocent and by the book, you wouldn't need the US Constitution, the federal courts, or the appeal process to overturn convictions that the state obtained from infringing upon the rights of American citizens.

This is part of the systematic predation power of the state government infringing upon the life, liberty, and property of the citizens within the jurisdiction of their control.

The problem is, so many people are falling or have fallen victim to it (self included) that don't realize what they're actually up against. I honestly don't fully understand what I'm up against. What I do understand is that it's powerful. It's tied into the roots of this country after it was extorted from the Natives. It's a well-oiled systematic machine that has countless technicians making sure updates are constantly being installed, so guess who can reign supreme? That can very well be a shallow thought pattern in the eyes of others, but at the moment, it's my thought pattern, and I believe it.

So if you think about the history of how the US Constitution was drafted and who drafted it, what type of white men drafted it? Their intentions when they drafted it? Who selected the fifty-five delegates? Why were they selected? Who were the 15 percent of white men who were allowed to vote? Why only those 15 percent, and how were the legislatures selected and not elected? You'll come to realize that what America has taught you to believe about Bloods, Crips, Latin kings, gangster disciples / growth and development, vice lords, P. Stone, MS-13, Mexican Mafias, Italian Mafias, etc. is nothing more than what America itself has been doing for centuries. Gangs have been guilty of countless homicides, extortion, money laundering, recruiting new talent for organized crimes, etc., but the US government has too.

Uncle Sam wants as much money from me, you, and everybody else as possible just to have puppets on television telling "we the people" that America is in debt. If America is in debt, then I recommend that Uncle Sam be drug tested expeditiously! Understand that I'm metaphorically speaking and fully aware that Uncle Sam is not a single person. Uncle Sam is just one out of many systematic procedures created by mythological white men with more power than mortals but less than a God.

This is the mind state of the people who drafted the law of the land. If you are a minority in the United States of America and you do not realize that we the people are endangered, then you are beyond sleep, brothers and sisters. You are in a coma! Not because of an accident. No! Your tragic mental state of mind is intentional. Those devils intended to keep barriers over our mental fortitude.

An accident is when something happens unintentionally. A mistake. If those slave owners who founded and framed the US Constitution made a mistake in all this, then this has got to be the longest mistake in the history of mistakes! In the words of my mother, "I might be a fool, but I ain't no goddamn fool!"

There were thirteen separate British colonies that we actually today call the United States of America. These thirteen colonies didn't want to be taxed by the British if they weren't represented by the British. That's understandable in my opinion.

My question is, how are we represented by the United States? They oppress us and then tax us for everything. Not only that but these thirteen British colonies have experienced firsthand what it feels like to be taxed, disregarded, and forgotten. Even to the extent where they declared their own independence in blood. Yet they used the same tactics even to a further extinct, to oppress us. These same founders and framers who drafted and fought for a Declaration of Independence were slave owners.

They took Britain to war, murdered them, and stole their concept to build the US Constitution (independence) they fought for. Yet when black people ran to escape slavery, obtain freedom, and to have our own independence, we were murdered by these same people. The Thirteenth Amendment says slavery is permitted in prison. When a person is convicted of a crime, Uncle Sam (the government) taxes them 10 percent on everything they purchase in prison.

The diabolical mindset of the people who structured and continue to structure the way America functions is just out of this world. Yet and still if you choose to use the same measurements that America has used to obtain its power, in the inner-city communities or suburban areas, it's frowned upon. It's a crime that's punishable by a significant amount of time.

The United States government labels it extortion, organized crime, RICO, etc. They label you as thugs, mobsters, rebels, hoodlums, terrorists, enemies of the state and United States. Forgetting all about how the United States itself obtained its independence on July 4, 1776.

Do you believe they forgot? Or do you believe they simply do not care because they have legislative, executive, and judicial branches that are put in place to confront people who possess an independent way of thinking outside the normality they structured in the supreme law of the land? Branches that are run by members of their elite group? Some of you may call these elite groups secret societies.

These elite groups / secret societies possess some of the greatest thinkers and influential people in the world. What or whom you may see as a hero, an idol, an icon, the pope, the president of the United States, congressmen and women, your favorite athlete, entertainer, singer, hip-hop artist, actor, or actress, etc. is possibly no more than a pawn in the chess game of life played by these elite groups / secret societies.

What you see on television is what they want you to see. What you hear on the radio is what they want you to hear. What you do is everything they allow you to do. So if your sense of hearing, seeing, and touching is being limited to what others have limited it to, then how much liberty do you actually have in the land of the free? How much independence do you actually have when you celebrate Independence Day on July 4?

Let's look at how the slave owners have structured the grand jury process. The elite groups are in a position of power to keep systematic procedures in motion. The grand jury process is equivalent to a whip, a lynching, or a gun line. It's a tool used to keep people in captivity against their own will.

The suspect in such a situation is not allowed to be present in New Jersey. If the suspect isn't present, how can he/she combat against accusations being presented against them? Your lawyer can be present, but he/she cannot interfere with the proceeding. What good is that at the moment when the state's counsel has the floor and complete control over the grand jury to influence them that you should be officially charged with a crime and/or crimes?

Evidence is presented to the grand jury that possibly would never make it to trial. Most of the evidence presented to grand juries to obtain an indictment is deemed inadmissible after the evidence has been questioned. Witnesses are cross-examined and most of their testimonies are deemed inadmissible as well. These things transpire *after* suspect(s) have been indicted and the pretrial motions have taken place.

You would have already been in the system trying to find a way out. Most of the time whether a person is innocent or not in these situations, they take a plea. They do this because they know it's an uphill battle that most don't win.

I'm telling you from experience that it's an uphill battle to keep slaves on the plantation. The only difference is, the plantation is no longer about color. Anybody can get it. It's about money, control, and order that stays strong and very much alive because of these elite groups / secret societies that think for less-fortunate thinkers.

When criminal defendants go to trial, the Sixth Amendment of the Constitution gives them a right to a fair and impartial jury. Ironically the judicial system is set up to give defendants the complete opposite type of jury.

Criminal defendants are to be judged by a jury of their peers. When the courts conduct jury selection, if there is a possible jury member who has a criminal background, they are removed. If they have someone in their family or close friend who has a criminal record, they're removed and cannot be a part of the jury.

On the flip side, if a person has family members that are police officers, they can be part of the jury. If they have never been accused of something, they can be part of the jury. If they are law-abiding citizens and pro police, they are more than welcome to participate.

The problem is, they believe everything the police say. Why? Because they have never had a run-in with them. So if the police hides evidence, covers up mistakes they have made, or when being cross-examined by defense counsel says "I can't remember," the jury will believe them.

When this happens, the defendant has the odds stacked against him. Here it is, a law enforcement officer can't remember pertinent information that will shed light on the defendant's innocence. They will say they have handled many cases since then and cannot recall the specifics of this particular case.

The jury will assume this is a law enforcement officer who puts his life at risk every day to protect and serve the community, and they will believe everything that comes out of his/her mouth.

Black's Law Dictionary

Social contract, or compact. In political philosophy, a term applied to the theory of the origin of society associated chiefly with the names of Hobbes, Locke, and Rousseau, though it can be traced back to Greek Sophist. Rousseau (contract social) held that in the presocial state, man was unwarlike and timid. Laws resulted from the combination of men who agreed, for mutual protection, to surrender individual freedom of action. Government must therefore rest on the consent of the governed.

When reading something like this, it makes me question, what individual freedom did Americans surrender? Are you aware of the individual freedom that you surrendered to be governed by the government? For you give them consent to govern you, shouldn't there be some form of written contract that is signed by you? Some form of legal document stating, "I John Doe of full age hereby give the United States government on the 15th day of January in the year of 2020 consent to govern me in exchange for the surrender of my individual freedom of action."

I never signed that contract, and I also don't remember anyone asking for my consent to be governed by them. If so, I would've asked, "Is this contract negotiable?" If it was, then tax evasion would have been at the top of my list. I don't know anybody who enjoys paying that shit.

Furthermore, if you think about it, no matter how someone may try to address it or clean it up, at the end of the day, you are born into bondage. You are born into a contract. You are born into procedures manufactured by a government that you unknowingly gave consent to govern you in exchange for individual freedom of action you never knew existed.

Think about it. They manipulated the system to strip this individual freedom of action from you in exchange to govern you and then you have to pay taxes to the government that's governing you. How is the United States of America capitalizing off this individual freedom of action? Do you really think they went through all this trouble if your individual freedom of action was not prosperous to them? I don't believe that for one minute. America was built off capitalism. What makes you think they are not capitalizing off us?

Let us discuss the mental aspect of prison

When people are arrested and spend a substantial amount of time in prison, they tend to suffer from posttraumatic stress disorder (PTSD) that society labels as institutionalized. Inside the institutions approved by federal and state governments, prisoners are becoming schizophrenic. Most are sociopaths and suffer from psychosis.

This mental illness derives from the development of prisoners living inside their mind to escape the harsh reality of conditions within the prison system. Prisoners suffer from paranoia, depression, loneliness, a subordinate mentality, lack of health care, always looking over their shoulder, and it is all manufactured by the systematic procedures set in place throughout these institutions.

Irreparable are the mental conditions of long-term prisoners. The punitive punishments that are bestowed upon prisoners with lengthy sentences are inhumane. There is no reform. Just a cell to rot in or an area to physically exercise. I've never seen a prisoner bench-press their way out of maximum security prison.

The lack of educational programs to obtain college education or even the opportunity to run a successful business from behind the wall is absurd (*in New Jersey State Prison*). How can prisoners better themselves as men and women if the normality of their condition is to be treated like a caged animal?

There is only one prison for women in the state of New Jersey. Clinton is what we call that facility. Those women were being molested and beaten by the officers. Many of them either have or are receiving law suits for what the officers have put them through. These are law enforcement officers who are doing this to inmates. If we can't trust the correctional officers in these facilities and have to always look over our shoulder, in regards to making sure we don't become another statistic, it will birth an edge to our personality. That personality trait now becomes part of the characteristics of our character. Which eventually will come out in our actions. We didn't plant that seed. Nor did we consciously add water to it. We just adapted to our environment.

We are disregarded when we strive to deal with self-preservation and elevate financially to take the burden off our loved ones. This prohibition prevents long-term prisoners from being responsible adults. Then when their conviction is reversed, an irresponsible adult that has done nothing except lift weights and develop a miserable and pessimistic mindset is released into society to accomplish what?

I personally have poor communication skills. I'm not a people person at all. It's not that I dislike people. I just find it more comfortable and less stressful being alone. I have been in and out of prison my whole life. Being confined did not rehabilitate me in any aspect. I got older, I matured, and I changed. I read a lot and applied the information I gathered, but prison has only taught me to mentally purchase real estate so I can live in my head to escape the physical conditions of inhumanity I'm forced to live in.

There are many times it can be difficult to pay mortgage, so foreclosure of the property I've purchased mentally will be at stake. This is when stress, anger, depression, and insanity sets in from not being able to cope with the reality of the circumstances we face.

Considering the conditions of the punishments we face plus the distant or broken relationships with loved ones turning their backs on us, can you blame us for having bad days or weeks? Waking up every day waiting to die. Knowing you were put here until you stop breathing. Seeing people in the prison who have been here for thirty years or more. Old men in wheelchairs who've been incarcerated since they were eighteen years of age. That reality frightens the toughest prisoners I've encountered. It personally frightens me, and I no longer hide it to portray a tough image.

I literally feel as if I'm locked inside of a casket that is buried under a mountain. Inside this casket I am scratching and clawing, trying to get out. Even if the judge reverses the conviction and the casket is unlocked, I'm still buried under a mountain. My next obstacle will be fighting for liberty from the county jail to remove this mountain. Sad part is, reversed convictions are not common at all amongst us.

Purchase a pet. Cat or dog. Let it live normal for two years. Then take that pet and lock it in a cage for six months. Do not let the pet out of the cage for anything. Let it eat, sleep, exercise, release its bodily fluids and digested food in the cage. When you clean the cage, transport the pet from one cage into another. No freedom at all.

Then after the six months, release the pet from the cage and see how it interacts with your other pets. There'll be abnormal aspects in the character of the pet. Possible high alert and trust issues. Better known as paranoia. When you call that pet to come to you, possibly it will run away. That possibility can be awarded to posttraumatic stress disorder.

If we are in agreement that six months of living in a confined condition will alter the mental condition of a pet, then we have to agree that years or decades of the same conditions affect the emotional and mental aspect of a human.

I'm unaware if animals have a conscious and subconscious, but I know humans do. Scientifically I'm unaware if animals have loved ones, like parents, children, or siblings they think of, but I know humans do.

So if the punitive damages for criminal convictions can tarnish a person mentally and emotionally, how is that fixing the problem? Is the justice system actually practicing a theory of torturing humans into repentance? That is a little extreme and diabolical in my opinion.

I am unaware of a religion that has a God warning people of torturing them into repentance. I mean, Satan has allegedly been in hell forever right? When is his/her release date? Is Satan addicted to pain and enjoys the torture as opposed to being in heaven? I have never heard of someone going to hell until they repent for their sins. That doesn't make sense. Allegedly everyone down there begs for forgiveness, but eternal fire means forever, right?

Torturing someone into changing is oppression. Oppressive were the slave owners who drafted and founded the United States Constitution. Oppressive are the three branches of the US government. Oppressed are the people who are governed by the government and have given up individual freedom of action in a social contract they are unaware of for protection.

A judge is the legal authority who enforces justice. If the enforcement of a judge is absent, people would be vengeful, without a care in the world of consequences. This was formulated by the judicial branch of the United States Constitution. Ironically a judge can administer justice legally without basing his decision on laws, yet if you look to obtain or actually achieve revenge outside the formulated procedure of the law, a judge will administer justice against you.

Is this part of the social contact,
Where Americans pay taxes...
and give up our individual freedom of action,
to be governed by the government's actions?
That's a mathematical fraction,
and the lowest common denominator is a disaster...
when you do the knowledge to their wisdom their understanding
is backwards,
controlling our culture with mental power because their
inequality is rooted in their actions...
But I'm a God who builds,
I born seeds of knowledge into the ciphers of the masses...
So when they knowledge my knowledge they'll put knowledge before
Wisdom,
that knowledge will give them an understanding of the country
we live in...
If they lack knowledge within their culture,
they'll lack knowledge of power which leaves them vulnerable
to vultures...
I knowledge equality and strive,
to influence the people to achieve knowledge and move like a
God...
So I knowledge the build while the government destroys,
I know the ledge of what's being born so I present wisdom to
your cipher and my word is bond...

Chapter 6

Convictions Based on Overwhelming Evidence

You've gone to trial. Your attorney has attacked the credibility of all the witnesses, the police, and has proven that eight out of ten of them are completely oblivious to the facts and are giving false testimony.

While the deliberation is going on, you are in a cell wondering if you'll walk or do a substantial amount of time in prison. You're thinking to yourself, *My attorney caught them in so many lies. There was no physical evidence in this case. I can't see how the jury will reach a guilty verdict. I should be in good shape.*

That is so far from the truth. The truth is, you had a defense lawyer, but did the defense lawyer really defend you? If so, what was your defense? Pointing out contradictions? That is only a portion of the battle.

You see, what we fail to realize is that the state called several witnesses on their behalf. Eyewitnesses, gun experts, doctors who performed surgery, the breakdown of the autopsy, family members, etc.

So when the state rests their case, which is the offense, your defense attorney has an opportunity to present their defense, which turns into your offense. Ironically the defense rarely calls in witnesses or experts on your behalf. The defense nine times out of ten will rest their case right along with the state.

If you are a convicted felon or have any prior misdemeanors, your attorney will suggest that you don't testify on your behalf. Why? The reason is if you take the stand and testify, the prosecution gets to inform the jury of all prior convictions you have.

If the jury hears that you have gotten arrested in the past for a simple assault, to them you are a violent offender, and it makes them biased to believe whatever the prosecution is striving to convict you of. Doesn't matter if someone smacked your girlfriend or little sister on the butt and you punched him in the face. The jury will never get the whole story. They'll only be notified that you have the potential to show a lack of respect toward the law.

This will ultimately make them biased. It will also persuade you not to testify on your own behalf because you know the jury will view you as one who has potential to participate in unlawful actions. Although you've already paid your debts to society, and the past conviction has absolutely nothing to do with the current matter at hand, the state's counsel will still use your prior bad acts against you to navigate the minds of the jury to reach a guilty verdict.

If you do testify, understand that you only answer questions. You do not lead the conversation and volunteer information. The state's counsel will object, and the judge will sustain it. Period! Doesn't matter if it's on direct or cross.

So you have all these claims made against you. Witnesses are coming in the courtroom testifying against you. Everything they say sounds believable. Evidence is being presented against you. You look into the eyes of the jury members, and they all give you blank stares. The judge won't give you eye contact. You look over your shoulder to see family support behind you, but your gut feeling says something isn't right, and then the jury goes into deliberation to decide your future.

After that you come back into the courtroom to hear a guilty verdict. You know they are about to give you a life sentence. If not, it'll be close to it. So you instantly become numb and bury the pain deep inside of you.

You show no emotion, although the world has stopped. You look back over your shoulder to see tears in the eyes of the woman you love, but deep down inside you know it's over because she will no longer wait for you. That is the reality of this situation, but you have no choice besides moving forward and enduring the pain to come with your poker face.

Think of it like this. You are in a championship fight. The jurors are handling the score cards. The prosecutor comes out swinging for twelve rounds straight. Your attorney blocks a lot of punches but doesn't dish out the same offense for the jurors to even consider a draw on the score cards.

In a unanimous decision. The jurors will rule the fight in favor of the state. Why? Because the state stayed busy the entire fight, overwhelming the defense with an abundance of offense.

In other words, the overwhelming evidence presented against you is what has swayed the jury members in favor of the state. You had a defense attorney, but you didn't have a defense that turned into an offense. So you went twelve rounds with your guard up, absorbing unnecessary punishment without using your jab to set up a combination. Of course it's overwhelming evidence. The fight is a landslide. You didn't fight back!

Do you think your attorney is unaware of these facts? I don't! He/she knows exactly what is going on. Yet they did nothing to stop it. This is the aftereffect of the smoke screen conspiracy!

Most of us don't realize we've fallen victim to it until we are sitting in a maximum security prison fighting night and day to see the light of day again. Sad part is, so many of us won't even pick up a book to learn how to get out. We'll just depend on another attorney to fix what's broken.

The appellate division has defense and state counsel as well as judges. That process is just as, if not more, impractical than the impractical justice you endured during pretrial and trial proceedings. In the next chapter, we'll discuss this topic in more depth.

Chapter 7

Appealing Your Conviction
In the past we fell victim to a genocide.
Today we mostly jump into the genocide not knowing the genocide
exists until victimization is felt.

After you lose trial, the world becomes dark and cold. The people who once said they loved and needed you no longer care and no longer need to hear from you again. You become a figment of their imagination. Dead to the world.

Friends disappear, family becomes distant, your significant other finds love elsewhere, your children learn to adapt to the cold world without you, and you feel helpless.

As you can see, this stuff will wrench a family apart. There is no difference in this, and the way our ancestors were snatched away from their families, except in modern times, we snatch and wrench ourselves from the people we love the most. We do it to ourselves.

In the past we fell victim to a genocide. Today we mostly jump into the genocide not knowing the genocide exists until victimization is felt. The game is cold! The problem is, we jump in the game to play it. This isn't a video game. You can't play life. Life will play you every step of the way if you allow it.

Back to the situation at hand. So you're forced to figure out all this stuff on your own. Your emotions, thoughts, and discomfort belong to you and you only. There is nobody to share these things with because nobody is there to listen.

My point is, when you get to prison, you're only thinking about getting out. People in the prison who have time in and are a little savvy with the law inform you to file a notice of appeal for direct. They start giving you stories about being time barred and how you only have a certain amount of time to put in for PCR (postconviction relief).

In your mind, you're thinking, *Even though my trial attorney isn't doing my direct appeal, he/she should have been obligated to at least put in for a notice to appeal the trial they lost.* Unfortunately, that does not happen. The judge will ask you at sentencing if you wish to appeal. You'll respond yes, sign a paper, and that's it. (In my experience, my trial attorney never filed a notice of appeal.)

When your trial is over, you are over. Your attorney forgets all about you the moment the case is finished. They'll know that you wish to appeal, but they will not have a secretary from their office notify the courts of it.

The notice of appeal is a form that is already logged into an attorney's laptop, computer, or flash drive. They only have to change names, dates, offenses, account statements, indictment numbers, etc. The whole process can be accomplished in ten to fifteen minutes. Why it isn't an obligation to them is beyond me. They have all the resources and tools to accomplish it in less than twenty minutes.

Apparently they won't do it, so you will sit in prison for at least a year, not hearing anything from the courts. You'll have to write the Public Defender's Office and request they have someone from their office to represent you and notify the courts that you wish to appeal.

Which is crazy because if you go to trial, obviously you plead not guilty. So if you plead not guilty, why would you not want to notify the courts that you wish to appeal the conviction? That should be an automatic procedure. Some of us may even consider it to be common sense.

Depending on what type of person you are, some of us quickly learned how to file a notice of appeal. In Trenton State Prison, many of us learned to memorize the formats word for word. We can file an entire notice of motion with a pen and blank papers, locked in a cell with no human contact, and nothing to copy it off of. Of course the criminal case information statement we don't memorize.

I personally filed my first three notice of appeals on my own. I probably was in Trenton State Prison for thirty days, and I quickly learned. The first time was denied by the clerk because I didn't put my middle initial in my name. I wrote the following:

State of New Jersey

vs.

John W. Die

in the captioned matter opposed to:

State of New Jersey

vs.

John W. Doe

The clerk sent my notice of appeal back stamped rejected. My soul dropped, and I panicked. Being naïve, I really thought I blew my only chance at direct appeal. The older men in the prison laughed at me and said, "Relax, youngin, you only have to correct your name so it matches the name on your indictment. The good thing is, you're fighting."

The second time it was rejected because I didn't have a six-month account statement. I was thinking, *I have not been here six months to have a six-month account statement.* I went to the law library, and a paralegal informed me to contact the county jail I just came from and request it. I did, and a few weeks later, I received it.

Both of those notices I filed pro se and personally handwrote them out word for word with no form to copy. I was on 4 Right at the time in the West compound, and my celly verbally told me what format to file it in. That was how I *first* learned how to write a notice of motion.

Keep in mind that during this entire procedure, you have no attorney unless you can afford a private attorney. When you call home, everyone asks, "Did you hear anything yet?" The more you say, no, the more they lose hope. So you're fighting mentally to learn the law, mentally to understand why everyone lost hope in you, emotionally not to lose your sanity, and spiritually because you start to doubt if there is a God and why he/she is watching you suffer day in and day out.

This is a dark and lonely journey for anyone to face. Understand and believe that it is designed to break you. None of this is designed to make you comfortable. You were and are an enemy of the state. That's why it says *State of New Jersey vs. Whoever You Are*.

Let us take a look at the procedure of appealing a matter

When you lose trial, you appeal the conviction to the *appellate division*. You would think you're able to argue everything in your case that went wrong so your conviction can be overturned. Absolutely not!

The fight is fixed, and the odds are stacked against you. They actually have rules to how you can defend yourself and fight back on appeal.

Say for example, in your discoveries, the crime scene photos show bloody footprints of the suspect walking out the back door. Those footprints, when measured, are a size 12 although you're a size 9. In trial, your attorney never argues this fact. Your attorney never presents the crime scene photos. Your attorney doesn't even call an expert witness for the defense.

So you lose trial, and now you want to appeal the conviction. The problem is you can't appeal any of those things. Why? Because direct appeal is for everything that is *on* the record. If your attorney or the state's counsel didn't mention these things in pretrial proceedings or in trial, it's not considered on the record. Which means you can't argue it.

You can only argue what happened in the courtroom. If there is a transcript of what was said in the courtroom, you can argue that all day on direct appeal.

If you have a private attorney, your trial transcripts will cost you $3,500 or better depending on how long your trial was. This price is *not* included in whatever your attorney fee is.

When the Public Defender's Office represents you, you have absolutely no say-so in your legal brief. Your attorney will gather your transcripts, send you a copy, and submit your brief to the appellate division without you even knowing what points he/she raised. You'll have to file a supplemental brief to add on to whatever he/she put in for you. Hopefully you know how to file a supplemental brief or you'll have to depend on another prisoner to do it for you.

If you lose direct appeal, then you appeal that decision to the Supreme Court of New Jersey. It's called a certiorari. The funny thing is, the Supreme Court denies almost every case that comes in front of them. So what's the point?

If you think I'm lying, try reading a *Black's Law Dictionary*. *Certiorari*—the Supreme Court denies most writs of certiorari (i.e., "cert. den."). The trend in state practice has been to abolish such writ.

That is not the entire definition, but that portion of the definition is definitely in there.

So if you have a state conviction and wish to appeal it, why is certiorari a part of the procedure if the Supreme Court denies most of them as a trend in state practice to abolish them? That just doesn't sit well with me.

Now once you lose the certiorari, you more than likely will have about four years behind the prison wall. So your next step is to file a petition for PCR (postconviction relief).

On PCR you can now argue everything that was off the record. Like ineffective assistance of counsel for not calling an expert witness to testify to the shoe size of the bloody footprints at the crime scene. You can now get the court to look at the crime scene photos. Your discoveries are now available for you to comb through and present to the courts—what your trial attorney should have done. The catch is, you *cannot* argue direct appeal issues on postconviction relief.

Take a look at what was previously mentioned above. You go to trial and lose. Your trial attorney doesn't file a notice to appeal. You sit in prison for about twelve to eighteen months before you get an attorney from the Public Defender's Office. Your legal brief for direct appeal is filed. Your attorney can only argue what's on the record, and you have absolutely no say-so in it at all. You lose your direct appeal, and then the public defender files a certiorari to the Supreme Court that you know nine times out of ten will get denied because of a trend. That is not justice!

The justice system is a systematic monster that will relentlessly eat you alive and spit you back out whenever it feels like it, if it even spits you back out at all.

Now you go to PCR and can no longer argue what's on the record. You can only argue what's off the record. You are fighting for your life! Kicking, scratching, and swinging everything but the kitchen sink at the courts to obtain your freedom, and the criminal justice system is enforcing a procedure that tells you, "You can wrestle the *first* round, but you can't swing closed fists or kick us. You can swing closed fist the *second* round, but you can't wrestle or throw kicks at us. You can throw kicks the *third* round, but you can't swing closed fist or wrestle us at all."

The fight is fixed, and the odds are stacked against you. They're prepared for whatever you're doing because they made the rules to the fight you're in. Purposely, certain things will be denied because they know it will open the door to other things to prove your innocence in the future. You're fighting for your life. If they wanted you to have it back, do you think they would make you fight for it?

To be more transparent on this topic, there are people from *all* ethnic backgrounds in here being dragged through the mud legally. Many of them have literally given up. They tore all their legal work apart, ignored any new bills that were passed, and accepted the fact that it was over. This is their home, and this is where they will die.

That's how dark and biased this fight is once you're behind the wall. We're considered to be the most violent prisoners in the state of New Jersey. Most don't care or are simply unaware of how impractical the justice system really is. It's not about what you know. It's about what you can prove, but if the system has the information and they withhold it from you, how can you prove it?

There is an anonymous man whom I've had the privilege of encountering with. His case is out of Hudson County New Jersey. He is amongst me now in Trenton State Prison. This man has been arguing the same point for twenty-seven and a half years. He's been telling the courts for almost three decades that he is innocent and someone else is responsible for the crime committed.

They kept telling him that there was no evidence in existence to support his argument. About fourteen years later, this man has had one remand and lost many appeals, so he requested his full discovery again. He went back to Hudson County, and his discovery was given to him.

Lo and behold the song this man has been singing for decades actually had a beat to it. They made the mistake of giving him information in that discovery they withheld from him all this time. Evidence that links someone else to the crime after they kept saying it doesn't exist. Exculpatory evidence best describes it.

Can you believe that after the exculpatory evidence came into existence, the same exculpatory evidence the state kept telling this person didn't exist, he still lost three more remands after that? That shows how corrupted the criminal justice system actually is.

The supreme justices couldn't believe how this information was overlooked, and this problem hasn't been resolved for all these years. This man is only one out of thousands who suffer from impractical justice. He still awaits for the decision as of May 6, 2021, and his fight will continue until he is free.

In August of 2021, the abovementioned person had his conviction reversed because of newly discovered evidence. His name isn't mentioned in this book because he is what some of us call a snitch, a rat, a sellout, and absolutely a *house Negro*!

He testified on his codefendants when he was in trial. Ironically, his testimony isn't what set him free. The sad part is, 90 percent of the prison population understands why he testified. Which only means 90 percent of the prison population are *house Negros!*

Chapter 8

Problems within the Prison System
More often than not,
I witness adults in the prison system
who have a desire to be *the* man opposed to being *a* man.
In prison you run across all types of people. People who are gang related. People who are religious. People who hide behind religion for acceptance or protection. People who use religious groups as a gang. Drug addicts, compulsive liars, manipulators, snitches, lip gangstas, homosexuals, thieves, intellectuals, etc. Boys and men is the bottom line.

What bothers me the most is when these adults act like children. Everybody *says* they *want* to go home, but very few *act* as if they *need* to go home. The few that act as if they need to go home are always mentally fighting the courts. You'll always know who they are because everyone will run to them for help.

Sort of like a child who runs to Daddy when something is wrong and they can't get past it. These are the gangstas who quote rap songs all day, lift weights, play basketball, smoke weed, get drunk, watch sports, talk on the phone all day, and strive to escape the reality of the systematic gangster who is whoopin' most of our butts relentlessly.

They'll quote a rapper who entertains people for money all day. "I'll shoot to kill and boot to grill," but if the state gives them an illegal sentence or violates their rights as an American citizen, they'll do nothing about it. The state can rip their families apart, shatter the hearts of their children, and the correction officers will disrespect them faithfully, but they'll do nothing about it. They're content with their circumstances. It's disgusting!

Very few will go to the law library and pick up a book to learn something. Very few will swallow a well-known enemy to man called *pride* and ask for help.

These are the guys who will pay someone to do all their legal research, draft all their motions, file them to the courts, and sit around doing absolutely nothing to get out of prison. Just because you paid someone to do your legal work doesn't mean you're fighting to get out. That means you're paying someone to fight your battles for you.

As I write this right now, at this very moment, I'm on my third paid attorney. I can promise you that I never sat on my butt and did nothing to assist them. I've written many letters, probably too many letters and got on their last nerve, but I honestly don't care. I *want* and *need* to get out of prison! My *conversations* and *actions* on a daily basis show where my mind and energy are at.

A lot of the adults in prison want to portray as if they are a boss. As if they're not bothered by the circumstances we live in. They have this "I don't care" attitude. I'm too thorough to stress or be upset with prison. Why you so miserable? Mannnn, kiss my entire ass!

You damn right I'm stressed! I have children and family. You damn right I'm upset and miserable! I'm sexually deprived, I haven't seen my kids in forever, they out there calling some other guy daddy, my mother just passed away, I'm teaching my nephew tricks about boxing over a damn telephone, I sleep in a cell the size of damn tuna fish can, and I'm surrounded by grown-ass children who don't understand the severity of the war we are in.

To these young-minded adults, you should have thought of that before you came to prison. Many of us weren't conscious before we came to prison, and I'm actually innocent. The real problem is, after all this time they gave us to sit down and think, many of us won't think at all. If we do think, it'll be something stupid.

We'll remember a professional basketball players points, rebounds, assists, and steals from a game fifteen years ago. We'll remember who was on his team, their points, rebounds, assists, and steals. We'll remember the opposing team's players and the same for them but *can't* and *won't* remember a rule or law that will help us get out of prison. That is a damn shame!

They are too busy putting on a front as if they are a vicious gangsta, but the real vicious and relentless predator is *the criminal justice system.*

Many of us come into these institutions not realizing that we actually are the prey. If we are predators, then the truth of the matter is, the predation we live by is self-inflicted. We bring upon our own demise, which is a form suicide in a sense. Unconscious suicide to us, but the seeds planted in our minds were consciously put there.

The younger generation has a premature mind that hasn't developed well enough to comprehend the fact that these entertainers are there to simply entertain us. Because of that, these undeveloped and premature minds are more than entertained. They start believing and following an entertainer who just wants to make a living. Ignorance is in high demand, so ignorance is what you will see all around you. There is no age bracket for it, and common sense is not common at all.

The things you entertain become a part of who you are. We often entertain all the wrong things, bringing negative energy into our own lives. Negative energy doesn't bring upon positive things. Negative energy brings upon more negative.

So here we are, in a dark place from making negative decisions, and we continue to push more negative energy toward each other. Then we wonder why nothing positive is transpiring in our lives. To understand this is to understand the mathematical and physical theory concerned with chaotic systems.

You see, there is a difference between a thug and a gangster. A *thug* has this "I don't care" mentality. I do what I want, when I want, and nobody better not say nothing about it. They can't think for themselves or others because they simply don't care. If they do care, they're simply not smart enough. Which makes them less-fortunate thinkers. They're more often than not emotional and act on emotions when things don't go their way. It's basically a childish mentality that has never matured.

A *gangster*, on the other hand, does care. They think for themselves and others. They don't do what they want. They do what they have to for the benefit of everybody. They make sacrifices and take personal losses to protect the ones they love. They are deep thinkers. They don't act on emotions because they're too busy basing their actions on *logic* and *principles*. They think for the future and not for the moment.

You know who some real gangsters are? I'll give you a few from my own personal opinion. Nelson Mandela, Malcolm X, Marcus Garvey, Harriet Tubman, Rosa Parks, the BLA and BPP, George Jackson, Bob Marley, Martin Luther King Jr., Jay-Z and Beyonce, Lebron James, Killer Mike, Kerry Washington, Barack and Michelle Obama, Tyler Perry, Dr. Dre, Ice Cube, Al Sharpton, Rihanna, Nipsey Hustle, Puff Daddy, Minister Louis Farrakhan, and I love that woman Eboni K. Williams. Every professional athlete who refused to participate in games because of the ongoing racism in America. The list goes on.

What makes these people, along with many others I didn't mention, gangster is they all thought for themselves and others. They made many sacrifices to get where they are and used their platforms for something positive. They put others in position to achieve wealth. They all have morals and principles. They all fought back mentally against whoever tried to oppose them.

*****

(Let me say this before you all get emotional and bent out of shape. When I say the abovementioned people are gangsters, what I'm really saying is they are heroes. They are people who make or have made a positive change with their influences on others. People who should be more admired for the work they've put in beside others who have led so many of our people to shame.)

*****

In court, it isn't a physical war you're in. It's a mental war between the defense and the state. You are mentally fighting for your life. Mentally, you have to understand the rules governing the courts. You have to understand the procedures. You have to know how to apply them and when to apply them. There is nothing physical about this war.

A thug, as I once was, would enter a courtroom and sit there not uttering a word. A nonchalant look on my face, leaning back in the chair, and really not understanding a damn thing those people were saying. The judge knew this, as did the state's counsel and defense attorney. But if I don't care, then why should they? Not like we're friends or family.

That wasn't the actions or thoughts of a gangster. That was stupid and yes, *I was stupid*. A gangster uses their mind. They figure things out. They stand for what they believe in. Thugs stand on emotions and premature thoughts.

Access to Law Library

In the current prison I'm housed in, the access to the law library works like this. You fill out a G-27 slip. In other words, a law library pass. You can either sign up for reading library, law library, ILA (Inmate Legal Assistance), request material, and request interview.

You have well over a thousand people filling these slips out. You're only one person. There's the West compound. Left and Right side. They go on different days. North compound same thing. South compound same thing. The law library is only open five days a week. How often do you think you'll get a chance to get down there and do legal research? If you make it down there twice a month, you are fortunate.

When you do get called to the law library, you only have about an hour to do whatever you need to do. That means you need to know what you're researching, how to find it, download it to a floppy disk, and get ready to leave. Unless the information you need is in a book. If that's the case, you have to be a quick reader and then ask one the of paralegals to print the case out for you.

So one hour maybe twice a month to research legal material to fight for your freedom. That's all you get. At least in this spot. That's not access. That's pathetic.

Outdated Machines

In the state of New Jersey, we are only permitted to purchase typewriters and word processors for our own personal use. So today it is May 5, 2021, and as I'm typing this book, I am in my cell at 8:49 a.m. using a word processor 5850 MDS. This thing actually has a floppy disk! No flash drive or CD but a floppy disk.

These machines are not even being manufactured anymore. The companies who do sell them to us charge a few hundred dollars. When you contact companies to get print wheels, it's almost impossible to find them. Society stopped using these machines decades ago, so nobody is manufacturing the parts if your machine breaks.

The internet wasn't in existence when these machines were manufactured. Can you imagine the limited dictionary on the spell-check? *Internet* isn't a part of the dictionary on the thing. Words like *isn't, shouldn't, won't, you'll,* or *hasn't* pop up as misspelled words. We are roughly forty years behind technology-wise trying to keep up with new case laws, bills, and court orders.

No laptops, no computers, no tablets with Lexus Nexus programs to research cases. No internet access at all. The kiosk is what we use to sync our tablets to so we can download emails, pictures, music, and books. No legal material though. We only have legal access to law library maybe twice a month if we're fortunate.

So these outdated machines are what we use to draft legal material to the courts. This is an uphill battle with the state at the top of the hill throwing rocks, logs, bottles, and garbage cans at us, while some of us continue to fight and climb to the top of that hill.

It's not easy. It damn sure ain't fun, but any real man or woman who dearly loves their family or themselves will fight diligently for what they believe in.

Not unless you want to wait to get into the law library or ask a paralegal to do it for you. But when your freedom is on the line and you have a real gangster mentality, you're not waiting on anybody if you don't have to. If you can do it on your own, you *will* because you have the *will*.

In the law library, they have computers. No internet access, but there are computers. Those computers have Lexus Nexus for you to do legal research to cite case law. You just can only purchase these outdated machines for your own personal use in your cell.

Books Not Permitted in the Prison

Ironically, the band list for books not permitted is unbelievable. Anything on Black Panthers, Black Liberation Army, or anything about the Negro Revolution is not permitted. This book will more than likely not be allowed into the prison system. Any book about any Negro who fought back and took a stand in the sixties and seventies is not permitted.

That isn't just Negro books either. Let's be very clear that every nationality has groups or individuals who are considered rebels. None of their material is permitted. If you admire Hitler, you better have a good memory or a great imagination because nothing on Hitler is permitted.

Most self-help books are not permitted. Robert Greene is one of my favorite authors. *The 48 Laws of Power, The 33 Strategies of War, The Art Of Seduction*, etc. None of his material is permitted. I assume they believe we'll use the information contained in these books against the officers. If that's so, then maybe the officers need better training.

Electrical books are not permitted as well. You cannot learn how to play with wires. That's considered, I assume, a threat to the prison. You also are not supposed to start a business in prison.

So let's take a look at this for a moment. Slaves weren't permitted to read back in the day. You can read today to elevate your mind. You'll just elevate as far as they want you to. The information you obtain is monitored, and the powers that be will decide what you're allowed to mentally process. That's not physical confinement. In here you're subject to mental confinement as well.

They say prison is to rehabilitate people so when they come back into society, they'll be better citizens. How? Prevention is set in place. If we read business books but can't start a business, we have to rely on someone from the outside world who believes in us to pursue our dreams, split the profits with them because they're basically running whatever you got going on. How are you getting rehabilitated?

Some of us don't have a support team. Some of us don't have anyone who believes in us. As I've mentioned earlier, this system snatches families apart. The longer you're in here, the more people forget about you. So if you're forced to figure it out on your own and cannot apply the info you obtained from reading to start your own business, what do they expect you to do once you're released? Work at a fast-food spot? Be a cook at a restaurant? Basically come home to slave for someone else because you've been slaving the entire time you've been in prison.

There are brilliant minds in prison. Brilliant! We have nothing but time to think. If you can sell drugs, dodge the police, instill fear in stick-up kids, keep close tabs on your team, stack your money, outstrategize your competition, and think well under pressure, you can run a business. A successful business at that.

The problem is, while we are in here sitting around wasting time, we can't apply this business mentality to start anything without the administration having an issue with it.

There are no college classes here. There isn't a paralegal course here from an accredited school. No degrees or license to obtain. So what are prisoners banking there freedom on once released? The jailhouse certificate that says you participated or completed the fundamentals of something. That's what we put on our résumés? Really? Impractical justice!

We Are Our Own Worst Enemy

I had to learn over the years to stop thinking something was
wrong with me because
I think and move different from others.

I wasn't the problem.

The problem was those who weren't thinking and moving as I was.

We are our own worst enemy in the prison system. The things we consider affect who we are and what we become. An illustration of this could be anything from the conversations we partake in, the quality of company we keep, what we're engrossed with on television, the thoughts we entertain, and who we think we are as opposed to who we really are.

The bottom line is, we don't have self-awareness. We are unaware of the self-imposed dangers we victimize ourselves with. We are unaware because it's cool to be ignorant. Which is contrary to what our ancestors fought for.

At one point in time, we couldn't read or write because we were not permitted to learn. If it became known that a Negro was learning how to read or write, they were killed or beaten to instill fear in other Negros not to follow his/her lead.

Then many decades later, after slavery, when we were able to obtain an education, Negros could not attend school with Caucasians. Could not read the same books, drink from the same water fountains, or eat from the same diners.

Once we were able to obtain knowledge after decades of many deaths, torn families, children auctioned off, and women being molested, it was our creative minds that built and solved many problems for this country.

Unfortunately, today our people have lost the *pride* we once had. We've lost our *unity*. We lost our *morals* and *principles* as a whole. Today it's cool to be stupid. It's okay to be unaware. It's accepted not to fight back.

When I was growing up, we had something to prove! My parents always told me, "When you go to school, let them folks know you just as smart as the rest of them kids and deserve to be right there with the best of them." I wish the hell I would drag my sorry ass in the house with a failing grade. My father would've put foot to ass expeditiously!

We were taught to fight back. You stood up for what you believed in. The community stuck together. All the older men and women in the neighborhood looked after the kids when we were outside playing. Any one of them would jump in your business if you did something your mother or father wouldn't be proud of. Then when you got home, your parents jumped in your business because you were their business.

Today our people are too content and relaxed in their current situations. So many of us don't want to achieve more out of life. The sad part is, we have so much potential. Untapped potential that could build generational wealth if learned and applied.

It's easy to be stupid. It requires no effort. Anyone can do that. That's why they don't give out Super Stupid Awards. It takes a real man or woman to use their brain and stand out amongst the elite. Are you a man/woman? Or a little boy/girl? Children are unaware because they have premature minds. What the hell is your excuse?

Many of us believe we are something that we're not.

Those of us who actually are what you want others to believe

you are strive to get away from it.

The younger generation or even the older generation will put on this act as if people should know better than to cross their path. They always have these war stories where they came out victorious. Or they mostly talk about what they're capable of doing.

Let me give you a precious jewel. Those types of people always get their ass whooped. They're not who they say they are. The most vicious people I've encountered are humble. Very polite and quiet. You'll never see it coming.

The history of these men and women is told by others. They never have to tell their own stories because everyone knows it. Being that they already lived it, it's no big deal to them, so they never speak on it. It's the ones who never lived it, have nobody to vouch for it, that have to tell their own stories.

The question is why? Why is it a necessity to be violent or outspoken toward your own people? Why is it a necessity to put each other down every chance we get? We are already put down and striving to get up from what we've encountered through the slave mentality. So in the mix of all this, we verbally put each other down and physically kill each other while our opposition sits back and laughs.

I'm not exempt! I'm guilty of it too. I've done many things that I regret now that I'm older and more mature. I've shattered the hearts of many black women. I've had many violent streaks in the streets of New Jersey against other black men. I've verbally abused my own people, and today I'm ashamed of it because I know I was speaking and acting like a house Negro!

Attention!

To every sister I've ever hurt or disrespected in the past, I am sincerely sorry for my past deeds. As a brother, I've disrespected you, neglected you, let you down, shattered your hearts, and have been a complete asshole.

I was not a man. I did not behave or think like a man. As a man today, I am ashamed. I am ashamed of how I shamed my sisters. I am ashamed of how I shamed my parents, who taught me to treat my sisters with respect.

Black women, I am sorry for every brother who's mistreated you. They are the most disrespected women on planet earth. Yet they are the most courageous, intelligent, beautiful, and confident women I've ever encountered.

If it wasn't for black women, there would be no Lebron James, Kobe Bryant, Magic Johnson, Jay-Z, Martin Luther King Jr., Malcolm X, George Jackson, Al Sharpton, etc. Black women have birthed all of us, and they deserve all our love and respect for eternity. I am sorry. I mean that shit!

Black man, brother, I'm sorry for every one of you I've physically hurt over the years. We have enough problems as it is, and I was wrong for contributing to the struggles we already face as black men in America. To each and every last one of you, as your brother, I am sorry. Yes, Jamar "Dro" McCoy is publicly apologizing to every brother and sister I've ever disrespected or hurt. Your forgiveness would mean the world to me.

*****

A person will hate you because you have the courage or willpower to do what needs to be done. They will envy you because they aren't strong enough mentally to do what needs to be done. It's easy to be foolish. It's the consequences of being foolish that are difficult to deal with. If you can find comfort in dealing with the consequences of being foolish, then you must be out of your goddamn mind! You're content with being stupid.

I had to learn over the years to stop thinking something was wrong with me because I thought and moved different from others. I wasn't the problem. The problem was those who weren't thinking and moving as I was.

The mentality in this place is like the "crabs in a bucket" theory. Everyone is pulling each other down from all angles. The ones behind your back, on the side of you, in front of you, etc. It can be a smiling face, a familiar face, a poker face, or a sad face that'll stab you in the back over the most minute thing in here.

You would think the mentality of the prisoners would be Us versus Them. Meaning the prisoners from *all* ethnic backgrounds should come together and fight against the state that has all of us confined. Unfortunately, that's not the reality of what is transpiring. It's really Us versus Us plus some of Us versus Us and Them! It's pregnant with so many house Negros and ignorant field Negros that real Negros are almost extinct!

More often than not,
we oppress each other with our own self-hate and ignorance.

Nobody wants to help each other or see one another be prosperous with anything unless they can benefit from it. The greed that lies in the hearts and minds of the people in prison is beyond pathetic.

For an extra tray of food or can soda, a house Negro will throw you under the bus in the drop of a dime. They aren't hiding anymore. This isn't back in the day when people stayed in the closet, so to speak. Those days are long gone! The closet door is open, and people feel free to be themselves.

The ignorant field Negro is almost if not just as pathetic to me as a house Negro. These are the ones who don't know anything, don't want to learn anything, won't do anything to achieve anything but want everything, show a lack of respect for everything, and will work your last nerve with ignorance.

They won't tell on you, but not putting your foot in their ass is a full-time career because their ignorance begs you to put foot to ass expeditiously. But deep down inside you know, no matter how much they work your nerves, they simply don't know any better. Grown-ass ignorant children with nothing on their mind except dumb shit.

I understand if you suffer from this. Whether you're in a facility for men or women. Ignorance is not based on gender. Ignorance is gender X. It's everywhere, like flies on shit. Let's just be clear about that.

If pride, ego, and the fake tough persona can be pushed to the side, we can accomplish more. If the self-hate mentality can come to a halt, we can accomplish more. Our people hate what we are not and will hate on you if we can't get what you have.

Unity isn't spelled H-A-T-E. We need unity to accomplish things as a whole. The Million Man March wasn't accomplished with one man. Malcolm X didn't accomplish everything on his own. He had unity with him. Muslims have unity, Christians have unity, and KKKs have unity. What the hell is our problem? We have got to do better to achieve better.

Unity is what got Joe Biden in office. Unity is what got George Floyd's killer arrested and convicted. Unity is what let America know that *black lives matter*! So unity is what we need to keep the ball rolling to achieve more.